WALK OF LIFE

...FRAGMENTS OF THE FRAGILE MIND

SAVIO J. S. PAES

This book is an attempt to tell myself that:

"Writing a book is possible and no matter how long it might have taken, YOU have finally done it"

It may be just the FIRST STEP, but a start is all you will ever need to get going.

I am **Indian,**

B U T

I am **also from GOA**

Hailing from a country like India and being Goan at the same time, is well...

...like going on a solo trip with a song on your lips and love in your heart –
Love for the Country & the State

Contents

Foreword

Savio and I have known each other since the beginning of 2019. I initially didn't know his name, but I had been reading his blog for a while, namely *"Goin' the extra... aaamile."* When I came across his comments on the blog posts of my fellow writers, I would say to myself; 'it would be nice if someday he could be a part of *"Candles Online"* too, my magazine on the web (webzine). And the day eventually arrived when I received an email from him, and the rest as they say is HISTORY.

Savio's command of the English language and overall presentation of a sentence or article are two factors that I can guarantee about his writing. His presentation, formatting, and writing style have literally won me over. He enjoys adding colorful titles and subtitles to his articles in addition to appropriate wording. having the ability to make a dry subject or article appealing so that the reader will read it and understand its underlying message.

The book "Walk of Life" is a very lighthearted book that is very relatable to all of us, as Indians. This book has it all in a nutshell, whether it is a discussion about Shahrukh Khan or a mundane story about everyday life. Some of the articles are also quite amusing. To cite one such example that caught my eye, was in a sentence where he mentions:

> *"...thank goodness for one thing at least, it is STILL the WOMAN who has the responsibility to bring new life into this world! Can you imagine if it was a man behind it!?"*

Some of the other articles that he has included in this book are quite insightful and thought-provoking. If the reader in 'you' find value in them, it will be extremely beneficial to daily life. It is definitely a feel-good book, and a personal copy will not only take much place in your bookstand but a definite corner of your heart in terms of bringing a smile to your face.

I congratulate Mr. Paes on coming up with the idea for this anthology of story-like articles. I wish and hope that the "Walk of

Life" touches the hearts of the readers and brings many accolades back to the writer, who deserves them all.

Chiradeep Patra
Digital Creator, Blogger & Author

Preface

To be an **Indian**... is a matter of pride. To be associated with a country, have a nationality, and most importantly to have a sense of belongingness to something, is a feeling everyone must enjoy, living on this Earth for 'X' number of years. I boast of an Aadhaar card, Pan card, and a Passport among other documents, stating that I am a fully bred INDIAN – but of course, nothing beats the feeling of being **A Goan!** Having people tell you that you are extremely lucky to be living in Goa, is probably one of the top 2 things every Goan will be proud of hearing every other day. It is also to be noted that not every Goan lives next to the beach (I certainly don't) and well... I also do not have a neighbor by the name of Anthony Gonsalves, I might have a Kumar or a Sharma for a next-door 'hello', but then they are equally friendly, kind, and warm. That is what Goa does to people who wish to make a home in the state, it transforms the ruggedness of an individual into the warm-hearted soul that the people of the state enjoy and is used to. That does not mean by the sheer fact of owning a house in Goa, the average Indian can take in the goan-ness and call themselves a Goan. It takes only a Goan to be one....and act like one, the rest are just cheap imitations, just like the jewelry one can find at flea markets sold by non-goans.

I was once told by a very intelligent man, found behind a stack of dusty books in a small library on the hill station of Ootacamund; on getting to know that I was from Goa. He said:

"Son, the success that you gain in the future will come from knowing the difference between you being an Indian v/s that of being a Goan at any particular moment in time"

I might have not understood what he meant by that exact statement on that day, but as I go motoring along life's journey, the words seem clearer and clearer. Profound words by a man who not only was a perfect stranger but also someone who by his knowledge and wisdom, saw something in the *'tired looking individual'* that once dared to enter into a dingy little room he called a library, probably his only visitor for the day, not to, particularly scout for a book to lend but to take a little time off from unusual hot sun blazing from the bright blue sky above.

While I delve into some of the few situations I have found myself in... a few of those memorable moments on travels, perfect strangers turned friends and the whole illusion of having to look for love in a loveless era... being an Indian, is simply an experience – the more one moves around, the more we understand how special it is to be an Indian, *still living in India even after completion of 4 decades of his life* – with no ambitions of migrating to the many of the 'firangi' countries on the globe.

What's India to an Indian and a mix of everything else in between... if there is something you can learn from this book, it will be:

"....there's nothing as the perfect country, it has to be a combination of a lot of adjustments, heartbreaks, and if you're lucky enough a few laughs as well. Adopt that kind of practice in your everyday life, and no day will be dull – there's too much happening on an everyday basis"

Savio J. S. Paes

Acknowledgements

To go ahead without taking a pause and think about those people who have in some way or the other – helped, appreciated, or pushed me to write, would be greatly unfair.

To God, for the talent of writing, he has blessed me with, though it took me such a long time to have it materialized and see it in the form of print.

My dad, who himself is the king of English vocabulary, and at many times - a constant back-and-forth discussion of father-n-son of which word can be used better in a particular situation, he has been the backbone of my love for English, the spoken and the written word.

My English teachers would have not imagined in their wildest dreams that, firstly I would someday teach the language and follow it with an attempt to write something worthy of a publish.

The Candles Online Family (a webzine) comprising of a bunch of enthusiastic writers, headed by the very simplistic natured - Mr. Chiradeep Patra, who not only pushed me to write, but his constant words of encouragement finally got me here, and I couldn't be more grateful.

For me to actually get work done, it takes a whole lot more than just encouragement, the push, drive, and determination among other things. Music as well, has played its part in motivating me and in telling me – ***You have it in you, Go for it!***

And while this book may never reach the hands of the singer Katy Perry, her songs have been such an inspiration in more ways than one – there hasn't been a single day that I've gone to sleep without having been told that I am a 'Firework' or that my life can be 'Electric'.

To Mum, Dad, and my sister – this book will show you that I wasn't kidding when I kept telling you *all* that;

You will see my name in PRINT someday

CHAPTER I

Look WITHIN you... AROUND you

One of the very first lessons we learn from our parents is to "look where you are going" ...and inevitably we never seem to forget that lesson as long as we live; be it crossing roads, bumping into people or walking in and out of doors. A lot of us still however are yet to master the PULL and PUSH parts of the door - without the actual stickers being pasted, we will eventually end up doing both and sheepishly smile to ourselves, looking around if we've been watched.

It isn't so much of looking around us that matter, but truthfully said, **it is what is within us is what matters the most.** Living in a country as big as ours, most of us do not actually get the time to ourselves, we find ourselves busy either at educational institutes, workplaces or caught up in the frenzy of the hustle bustle of life that leaves us with less **quality time by ourselves.**

When was the last time you took a trip by yourself? Had a heart-to-heart conversation with someone? Or simply spent a quiet evening looking at the sun set doing nothing else?

I'm sure when I speak about myself, I am not one that considers myself not too much of a thinker, hence the average thoughts that would occupy space in my mind would be getting myself from one location to another (which is looked after by my personal vehicle), the food that I would consume and the money that I will earn at the end of a particular period. That's about it, can't get any simpler than that right? ...and of course, the constant thought of when will I be a published author!? If this finally makes it to print, that will be one less thing to think about.

We are a bunch of people walking through life's journey with a lot of baggage, if you're an Indian traveller, you'd know. We're all scarred in some way or the other from the inside... we go about this life searching for a solution, an outlet – at best someone who can understand us for who we are. Who are you zeroing in on...?

• • •

CHAPTER II

Single in the city

Singles want to get hitched; the married ones want to be single again, the divorcees are busy relaxing and advising... it's all about the concept of **"the grass is always greener the other side"**
How is it that then ...some of us - all we can see are pebbles?
Where is even the grass?
I used to hear this phrase a lot, said by a friend of mine in college
"catch them young and watch them grow"
...as catchy as this phrase sounded to me, it didn't quite strike a chord. **I was wise enough to know what it was in reference to, but probably equally scared to follow its path.** On meeting this particular friend after many years, I got to know he had planted his seeds all over the place, not sure if he even got to watch over them all, while here I was - I was yet to find that 'one flower' which I would have liked to bloom myself.

If there's anything harder than passing an exam, it is finding **true** love or even the simple kinds... and to think we live in a country of over a billion people! Wow! Being single doesn't look as easy as it seems... **we all want that someone to share our morning coffee with, someone to tell us that the shirt we're wearing doesn't suit us and that we need to change it, or simply someone to yell at us to say that I need a shave or a haircut! Somebody to accompany me while watching horror movies, eating pizza, and reading a book. Someone who would ask us about our day, someone to care about... someone who would be afraid to lose me.**

And for many of us, the saddest fear comes creeping in that there's a decent chance that any of this might never happen, yet there is always one thing that will spur us on and keep our hopes alive...

• • •

CHAPTER III

I am the NEXT Shahrukh Khan

Don't we all absolutely adore our film stars in India? ...in trying to imitate their dialogues, and dressing styles and even maybe shake a leg or two in the same way? We all have our favorites-from acting skills to perfectly shaped bodies.

Bollywood movies have made us happy, laugh, shed tears, and even left us depressed and heartbroken at times... I've also once come out of a movie theatre so reluctantly, as I found myself so attached to that particular story that I did not want it to end and come back to reality, and that's when you know you've truly been witness to a great piece of movie-making. However, the one thing that Indian movies do best is to play on the emotions of their viewers, and while I consider human beings generally to be a bunch of emotional fools (especially us Indians) people exit theatres thinking that they could actually live that kind of life in the real world. I'd be lying if I said that I didn't dream that same night, I was shaking a leg with Alia Bhatt or shaking booty with Deepika Padukone, or even romancing my girlfriend on the campus of my college. After all, dreaming is harmless, it is only in dreams that all those unfulfilled wishes are given wings to fly... and maybe someday it may even come true who knows!

From Sharukh Khan's iconic dialogues to Salman Khan's action-packed roles, there's a little something for everyone when it comes to a few hours of relaxation and time with friends and family. Along with watching a few hours of various actors and actresses entertaining us, we are unconsciously making movie reels in our heads, stories are being formed, character roles are being developed and out of all this comes out fresh ideas... ideas that make us proud, where we tell ourselves; I can write a story too, someday maybe I would direct a film or at best write a book. I've had that dream for the longest time... I am going to write a story. I'm never really out of ideas, all I need is a pen and a pad strung around my neck to write when inspiration hits, maybe in the middle of a traffic jam or while having a shower.

Why doesn't inspiration ever strike when I'm free-I wonder!!??

• • •

CHAPTER IV

The storytellers... in plenty

This has to be my favorite part, weaving stories out of simple observations is a skill I possess in plenty. Goa provides the beauty, the ambiance, and the picturesque setting to write these stories. It could be waves simply dashing onto the shore or a little girl cycling down the road... from neighbors screaming their lungs out to a young couple trying to get comfortable in a car – all one needs sometimes, is to have an eye for looking at things with a positive angle with a streak of humor and you are good to go!

"...me writing this story, you reading it in the comforts of your bedroom, with the a/c turned on to 'snow-mode' on a hot sunny day, and a dog licking the palm of your hand, while the pressure cooker whistles away in the kitchen.... little drops of condensation begin to drip from the cool drink that lies on the table, threatening to make its way into the laptop kept close by...."

See what I just did there? I created something out of nothing... Could that be something one could work with in terms of a situation, background and character portrayal?

Weren't we taught in school that all stories had happy endings? Well, reality showed us the practical side to those similar stories... but how about if a story did not have an ending... but was left to the reader to come to their own conclusion – now that suits everybody, doesn't it?

If people aren't busy making babies, they are definitely writing stories... I'm sure even as you turn to the right or left of your current location, there's either a baby being born somewhere or a book being launched.

As for the rest, they're playing games

• • •

CHAPTER V

Games People Play!

The phrase 'Games People Play' always reminds me of the song of the same name sung by the Band-The Inner Circle in the 90s, probably the only time that people actually played games in the correct sense of the word! ...and boy! did we enjoy those kinds of games? You can't blame me, I was still a teen back then and games to me meant Cricket for an outdoor sport, while UNO and Carrom made up some of the indoor games that I indulged myself in.

Life does however have a way of kicking one in the nuts or simply where it hurts the most, when somewhere down the line in life... "you" understand that the people around you are busy playing their own different kinds of games and then a situation like that happens to cross the simple life that you've been living until now – we are hit with what seems like a very complex maths equation, we know that we will get to the answer but it takes time to solve that particular problem. And as it is said, the longer something takes, the worse it gets – until you find yourself so far away from the solution that things have already gotten messy by the time you have thought out of an action plan.

To quote Cliff Richard (singer) in a couple of verses in his song 'Some People'

Some people they tease one another
Take pride in themselves
Keeping the other one down
Well, I'm not like that at all...
Some people they hurt one another
They love to see
Hurt in the other one's eyes
Well, I'm not like that at all...
Some people they use one another
So aimlessly

Not like lovers do
Well, I'm not like that at all...

Have you ever had a song speak to you in a way that it is trying to say something to - you - you've always wanted to hear? The thing with people playing games with one another is that there is always going to come out a winner and a loser. Unless you find yourself psychologically and socially inclined there is no way a game is ever going to be played in the right spirit. The trouble and time that people take out from their daily lives to indulge in activities such as these are to be appreciated. Of course, we learn more as we meet and move around social circles, because why not; if they can do it...

• • •

CHAPTER VI

I can do it too... subtly

I can do it too! The art of being a human comes with the ability to be yourself at home but a totally different person in social circles. We as human beings have got to be the most complex of existing creatures living on this planet, we hear something as simple as a piece of information, interpret it with large amounts of strategic thought processes and vomit it out to the next person available with the reasoning that defies logic, understanding or at times even proper comprehension.

Goa brings to us, the local goans, a sense of freedom while living in the smallest state of the country, it goes without saying that nothing can ever remain a secret in a goan household, however much we try to keep it within the four walls of our house. The charm of living in the state of Goa is living in close proximity with the neighbor, the sharing of information, gossip, and the everyday local happenings... sometimes as close as on the opposite side of the boundary wall. With larger families comes a lot of drama, and with a lot of drama comes spicy news – no better time for a hear-in to what may be interesting news that can be shared with relatives, friends, and over-enthusiastic gossip spread across the length and breadth of Goa.

However, the one thing we do not indulge in is 'physical fights', we would rather use well-crafted words in the local language to have our say, simply because no matter how much the language of English might have evolved over the years, having his say in the local language adds to the excitement and better expression of feelings – thus making a very ordinary situation sound fairly dramatic, 'we' are after all known to very expressive by nature.

• • •

CHAPTER VII

English ON SALE

No matter how much of an educated Indian you might be in terms of skill, passion, and overall smartness, life isn't quite complete if you don't find yourself being able to have a decent conversation in the international language of English. You WILL be judged on the basis of how well you are able to speak the language that is, by and large, looked upon as the Universal language of the world. I am sure if 'English-the- language' was a person, he'd be the most popular celebrity across the nations worldwide. India and its obsession with English goes a long way in trying to prepare the present and future generations to communicate in a language that not only sounds classy when spoken but is also understood and often mistakenly referred to as the second language of a particular nation. It is ironic, however, that in a country of over a billion people, the head of the country (The current Prime Minister) still chooses to address the nation in a language not totally understood by every Indian in most households. We are taught Hindi along with English and the local language in a particular state that we live in, and yet somehow English is given preference over the other two, not that I am complaining! I personally feel much freer to talk in English in comparison to the national language or even in the state language (Konkani) which at best I would say is more of an apology.

Of course, the fun lies in the mix of the different languages, and with the influx of domestic tourists spreading far and wide across the country, no language is safe when it comes to speaking it - we are all a product of a combination of English vocabulary, Hindi words and the local influence, throw a little bit of unsteady grammar and you have the package for a fun conversation.

The fact is everything and everyone is so drawn towards similar things nowadays: be it lifestyle changes, self-improvement, clothing styles or simply wanting to be as confident or competent as the person sitting next to us for a job interview or next to in the double seat in a bus...that we tend to sometimes overlook the whole concept of gender stereotypes – almost everything you are, I want to be that too.

• • •

CHAPTER VIII

U–n–I Sex

If you look around your surroundings, you can find a sense of sameness, its almost like people are literally going about copy-pasting each other into themselves – male and female are found visiting the same unisex salons, men are now doing facials, while women are the ones *'wearing the pants'* in their respective homes (literally and figuratively). Jobs that once women thought they were good at, men seem to have got one step better... **thank goodness for one thing at least, it is STILL the WOMAN who has the responsibility to bring new life into this world! Can you imagine if it was a man behind it!?** A lot of things might have interchanged in terms of life in general, things and situations that men and women find themselves in together, but what the world needs more of; is **a woman's touch and a man's bravado** when a particular situation presents itself, and not the other way round.

From unisex clothing to hairstyles, it all boils down to one's choice on which way to go, but what happens when it gets difficult to recognize a particular individual on which way, he/she swings – and I am not even referring to a particular gender here. Allow me to reiterate the same in the form of something I happened to be part of... I was very recently introduced, (not in the literal sense) to this person, where I went from: 'I think it was...' 'but it wasn't..' or 'it might be to 'I'm not too sure....' but how do I find out? It would be rude to ask directly. A classic example of 'unisex is cool and all...': but to what limits does one need it to be pushed? Living in the modern world gets tough when simple tasks get complicated and while the complicated tasks still need our attention, it gets pretty much muddled up – and for someone like me, I like to keep it simple – I call it as I see it, but of course, what I see needs to be clear, or else that is a problem in itself.

For the **U – n – Isex** to happen, it is necessary for the 'you' and the 'I' to find each other in the u-n-i-s-e-x world we currently live in.

I am ready, where are **YOU**?

• • •

CHAPTER IX

Friendship and Love

I am busy be-friending you.

The famous SRK dialogue comes to mind:

"Pyar dosti hai, agar woh meri sab se achchi dost nahin ban sakti, to main usse kabhi pyar kar hi nahi sakta, kyunki dosti bina toh pyar hota hi nahin, simple, pyar dosti hai, love is friendship..."

What can I say, as young kids when the movie came out, we were terribly influenced by this one particular dialogue that made us believe that love is friendship and one needs to be friends to fall in love.

Going by that logic, I have always been in love with someone or the other: friends, teachers, colleagues, neighbors, etc. The way Shahrukh Khan defined Love in that particular movie, anyone with a beating heart would fall for it, and I am sure You and I are no different in that aspect: after all, it did make sense to some extent.

Finding a friend might seem the most natural thing to happen to a human being, however building a feeling of love in him/her, has got to be one of the hardest tasks that mankind has had to struggle with for years on end, and it only gets more difficult living in a world that sees test drives being taken as a preliminary check to see if two people are compatible to each other in certain aspects, after which one can say with confidence "let's give the LOVE thing a try".

Do people enter a friendship for the sole purpose of seeing where it leads or is it because of mutual admiration for one another?

Whatever it may be: friendships are key to living a life worthy of happiness and success, if the same journey-it finds its course into TRUE LOVE, consider yourself the luckiest person, coz that is a rare phenomenon in the world we live in today, and you MY FRIEND are indeed truly blessed. Friendship plays by the rules of *give and take,* while when it comes to Love... it works differently.

• • •

CHAPTER X

I am ALWAYS here for you, BABY... Listen to me... I am talking

Aah! *the honeymoon phase... the fresh fragrance of newly found love, the closeness, the proximity, and the never-ceasing smiles found on faces* – a sight to behold.

Falling in love has never looked better on me, I am beginning to fall in love, with LOVE, he said

...and I smiled, it was evident that it was his first time.

The understanding of the emotion is felt in different ways, while some go the cute and romantic way, others feel the need to educate their partner in a way that will help both come to a better understanding. A simple accessory could look beautiful on a partner's body, however, on the other hand, a well-educated lover plays an equally important role in making a relationship work. What kind of **LOVER** are you?

So diluted is the whole concept of emotion these days, that as much as we are in love or think that we are in a relationship, the fact remains that it is still to be expressed to another person to be understood completely. The feeling of being addressed <gender neutral phrases> 'baby' or 'babe' is to date considered as cute. I wonder if there's a time when it would be normal to address loved ones with such phrases while Sir and Madam would be used in professional circles – sounds like a good plan going ahead.

No restrictions of course – you can still be *honey 'd or cutie 'd* on the intensity of how much one is liked and desired by another individual. I swear that I once heard a woman comment *'Hubba Hubba!'* on looking at a man shopping in a mall in Goa... and since a term like this isn't regularly heard in normal everyday conversations, I looked around to see the man, hubba hubba 'd, and I though **eh!** she could do better! And I looked at the woman again

"Hubba Hubba to you missy!"

Girls, listen to me – no matter how many times you are baby 'd into getting work done, it still takes 'you' to set the right direction your man needs to go, so while you're being all cute and romantic, it is also important to go ahead and say;

Listen to me... I am talking

And Men this one's for you; if the talking gets a little too much and your head begins to spin a little...

slowly walk up to her from behind, turn her around gently and kiss her *(now if you are Indian that will take a little bit of practice)* that ALWAYS works – put the dopamine, oxytocin, and serotonin hormones to work now... will ya!?

• • •

CHAPTER XI

The Journey... Indian Railways

There isn't a place or a moment defined where one can find love, it could be staring right into your face and you wouldn't know. However, when one is found to be in a more relaxed environment and surrounded by strangers, our senses are suddenly heightened, which may pick up certain signals, that may or may not be signaled directly. If you are a body language enthusiast, you'll know exactly what I'm talking about.

They say if you have found love for an individual on a particular undertaken journey, more so on an Indian train on witnessing a person's behavior – that love is real, keep her! We would all have to admit that traveling on the Indian railways, not only brings out the best and worst in us in terms of going through various emotions, it also brings out a side of us, that we aren't particularly proud of... but then again it is all the experience of being an Indian. We may be from different parts of the country traveling in a single compartment of a train, one is never short of expressing himself in the loudest way possible, while it may sound irritating to some, it is music to the ears of another. Why people carry and read books on a train to keep themselves entertained is beyond me, people seated around us are enough entertainment in themselves.

Indians can be entertaining, especially when it comes to music, conversations, and food. I will go one step further to that say food is by far the most common unifying factor that bring Indians and people together. I cannot recollect a single journey where I would have not shared a cup of tea sponsored by a fellow passenger or eaten a home-made chutney sandwich, which of course is only the start to a long conversation to follow. For some strange reason, life stories are exchanged to an extent where in – do not be surprised if you find an invitation card to their son or daughter's wedding once you return home. That is how beautiful journey's can be, from a simple conversation over sipping hot piping tea to building relationships and lasting friendships.

I haven't been the luckiest in terms of finding myself amidst an intellectual stimulating conversation with someone from the opposite gender, however I cannot complain that the company I've had on journey's hasn't been all that bad, even though it hasn't all been with the fairer sex. I gradually realized that hopefully reading a good book would entice some inquisitive girl to ask me about it... and from there we could... you know... if not get to know more about each other, at least discuss the book in detail. I'm still waiting for that day...

For other times, there is always the odd aunty or uncle to keep us occupied and busy with topics that do not necessarily interest us.

Who are you calling Aunty!? I am not your mother's sister!

Am I?

v/s

Aunty mat kaho na...

If you haven't been already been told off as yet... I suggest you quickly make the necessary changes and start addressing people the way they like it...

Just like you can do to me – Call me by my first name: Savio

• • •

CHAPTER XII

Age is just a Number

This a phrase people commonly use post the age of 30. It may be rude to ask a woman's age, but then it also doesn't change the fact that with every birthday we celebrate we're getting wiser and turning grey 'er in some cases white as well. No more are we made more conscious of the fact that we are getting older than when around children!

What happened to today's youngsters addressing people by their names? – why does everybody elder than them have to be an uncle or an aunty? Surely addressing another person by their name is still very much in fashion. **No Uncle... No Aunty.** If you do not know me, there's a word you can use to attract my attention, **'Excuse-me'** works well. It's indeed fun when people think they're growing old, solely based on a number that keeps advancing every year by ONE. I know people who are still active in their 70s while a healthy 45-year-old might think otherwise. **You are ONLY as old as you feel** and going by that measure, I still would like to believe that I am no more than a 25-year-old in heart, body, mind, and soul.

Besides a lot of my female friends say, **boys never grow up!** A man is still a boy in every way possible until he (or his mother) finds himself a wife, in some cases even that isn't enough. But of course, that depends from individual to individual, no judgments here. I guess then, post marriage one is qualified to be called an Uncle and Aunty? In that case – I am safe; bachelor and unmarried until now.

With four decades of my life completed, having spent all of them 'in the single status' – life keeps throwing examples of what it *could have been* if it was on the other side, looking out, and while the idea of it seems very enticing, the reality is far from it. The principle of my life has been simple: take one day at a time, even if it means you've already gone through 14,903 days and counting (you didn't expect me to do the math all by myself now, did you?) add a few more days until this book is published and the wait gets longer. The more you focus on the number, the unhappier you will be... live and let live, because the good news is...

Men never grow up, but WOMEN... do in fact grow OLD

'Old wine in new jars': women re-inventing themselves to look younger versions of themselves is the latest trend, thanks to beauty products that serve as age-enhancement tools. Since we have already drawn to the conclusion that Men never grow up, they're always looking around for greener pastures. The fact that women age gracefully is true, however, looking beautiful has always remained a WOMAN's top priority. No matter what a man says to the woman he loves, he will always have eyes to look, in the hope of sounding genuine and truthful with his words matching the view.

Being a man, we are in the endless loop of memes made of the other gender, as will be the same for them looking at us microscopically through the eyes of a woman. At the end of the day, we still must co-exist with each other, and the faster we learn to do that, irrespective of a number that defines us as an individual, the more we live in harmony and enjoy the other for what they bring to the table.

• • •

CHAPTER XIII

I am Me...and I wouldn't change for the world

The life I have led up to now, is a direct reflection of how I've been brought up by my parents and the education they've provided me through my formative years, and I couldn't be happier – to say that, though I might have not lived up to the true expectations of the person they named me after - 'St. Domnic Savio' and the kind of life that he led, I have turned out to be more like the kinds that is either in your face or totally missing – there is no in between and there will never be.

One cannot stress more on being yourself in today's world, where we find people adjusting their lifestyles according to the tune and patterns of what the world expects them to be. If you are one person, who has refused to budge on the values and cultures imbibed in you from your parents, state and country, be proud of yourself, give yourself a pat on your back. Someday we shall meet and talk about it.

It is also said that the people we come across and interact with on an everyday basis, play as much of an important role in one's life, as the family and relatives we are surrounded by. There is so much of positivity to take in from the world and the people around us, however, we MUST NOT ignore the fact that there will be those thorns along the way that will cut, bruise and destroy us bit-by-bit in taking away our ability to be ourselves and concentrate on the worldly pleasures instead.

Be careful...

There's so much to be grateful for; friendships, Love from special people who come to our lives for a reason and those unsung heroes who don't take credit for the kind souls they are.

Spread across borders of state and country, you know who you are! It is from people that we truly care about, comes the feeling of being together through prayers, thoughts and good wishes.

Be **YOU**.

And I will be **Me.**

Let us make the **You** and the **Me** meet someday, over a glass of cold coffee on a day of *hot Indian summer heat*, preferably in a shack somewhere on a quiet Goan beach – You and Me... making memories.

• • •

Epilogue

Our lives are a series of stories waiting to happen, and it would only be fitting if these 40-odd pages of writing concluded in a wonderful story itself... albeit fictional, but in a life with surprises at every curve – you might just be walking into one you'd least expect...

She asked him *"So what's our story going to be like"?*

He replied, *"we'll get married, and have 3 beautiful daughters all of whom will have your cute nose and curly hair..."*

"and your eyes" she interrupted, *those eyes when you look at me...*

The story didn't quite pan out the way they had imagined.

They paused a while and smiled at each other as they crossed to get to the other platform to catch their respective trains.

"Who was that Mumma?"

"Just a friend" she had said

She turned back to look, as I waved out my hand. She had her mother's cute nose just as I had thought

...so where will our story take us?

You know, like everyone has a story and when we meet others, our stories meet and continue...

No matter how long or short our stories may be..there will always be a story to tell of the two of us. Living in the same country, sometimes in the same state, from exchanging ideas to sharing little incidents of life, laughing at some, serious with others.

Does the story end there?

No, it certainly doesn't..there are no bye's in life because *yeh zindagi bahut lambi hai* (this life we live is very long)

What's your story going to be like?

• • •

9 798888 498781